the

flood

poems by CHIWAN CHOI

tía chucha press
los angeles

Printed in the United States of America

ISBN 978-1-882688-39-5

Book design: Jane Brunette
Cover painting: Nathan T. Ota, entitled "Alive"

PUBLISHED BY:

Tía Chucha Press
A Project of Tía Chucha's Centro Cultural, Inc.
PO Box 328
San Fernando, CA 91341
www.tiachucha.com

DISTRIBUTED BY:

Northwestern University Press
Chicago Distribution Center
11030 South Langley Avenue
Chicago, IL 60628

Tia Chucha Press is the publishing wing of Tia Chucha's Centro Cultural, Inc., a 501 (c) 3 nonprofit corporation. Tia Chucha's Centro Cultural has received funding from the National Endowment for the Arts, the California Arts Council, Los Angeles County Arts Commission, Los Angeles Department of Cultural Affairs, Los Angeles Community Redevelopment Agency, the Annenberg Foundation, Thrill Hill Foundation, the Center for Cultural Innovation, the Middleton Foundation, the Panta Rhea Foundation, the Attias Family Foundation, Not Just Us Foundation, the Liberty Hill Foundation, Youth Can Service, Toyota Sales, Solidago Foundation, and other grants as well as donations from Bruce Springsteen, John Densmore, Lou Adler, Richard Foos, Adrienne Rich, Jesus Trevino, Tom Hayden, Dave Marsh, Mel Gilman, Denise Chávez and John Randall of the Border Book Festival, Luis & Trini Rodríguez, among others.

table of contents

1. the dim light i hold in my cupped hands

2. damsel and plastic and blue blanket winters

3. speak to god in accents

1

in the

dim light

i hold

in my

cupped hands

architecture

i have taken to building in my sleep,
starting with small things—
a shelf for all my elephants,
four-feet wide and a foot deep,
with four legs six-inches tall,
a dining room table,
a new engine for my car.

today
i have built a mansion—
ten stories high,
stairs,
walkways,
bridges,
up and down and
sideways,
connecting everything to everything.

there are people in my architecture.
they walk in and out
of all the rooms.
i sit in the smallest room
with the comfortable green couch
as a woman tells me
of a song about a boat

that she used to listen to.
and holding my empty glass,
i tell her that i know that song
and sing out the lines about
the monkey taking his wife overboard.

i get up and walk to the bar,
turn back to see her cross her legs,
the left over the right,
smile
as she waves,
and i pour it full
with thick red wine
made with young grapes
and blood of bulls.

i take a sip
and walk out on a bridge,
look down at the house i have built,
the work of my hands
that remains beyond
comprehension.

after the war

give me one moment
for penance
on this rooftop over our city—
no more words written in red,
on my knees
hands empty
fingers free—
to pull such pieces of glass
so small
from her pale arms spread out.

we will count
each fragment
until i mistake her
for jesus
until she remembers
her father's house
and how slow and quiet
his pants fell past his aching knees.

los angeles dies below us
while we search for faith
in the scars on our chests,
the one under my left nipple

that she measures
with her tongue,
asking each other for destruction.

she says choke me
and i do
as she wraps her legs around my right thigh.
i hold her tight by her throat,
her mouth at my ear.
that is breathing.
i hear breathing.
i will hear her breathing
after the war.

blades

there is a beige two-story house
up my street on bronson avenue
and before the sun
i walk to it and stand
outside in the dark holding
my two dogs by their leashes
until they grow impatient
and lick the grass blades for
the dew that quenches their thirst
and i look up at the three small lit windows
of the bathroom
my free hand rubbing
the belly under my shirt
and watch for the person inside
sometimes a woman
sometimes clothed
and washing her face a little
getting ready for the day
of work and family
and disappointed romances

my mornings
each one
begin on my feet in the dark
looking for

a life
a window
a house
a second floor
a face
that is not mine
and once
on a saturday
the woman naked and the curtains open
stood at the window
turned toward the street
and i couldn't see her face
but she stood there for
five or six seconds
until she closed the curtains
and i walked on

and in the afternoon
i sit in the car on beverly headed east
and my girlfriend turns
on the wrong street
and as she drives in circles
she regrets not dumping me three years ago
and her friends are telling
her that i am not the right guy
and i say
i told you to turn the fucking car on virgil
and we don't speak anymore through
the ride

this broken body
can't hold the sparrow
of the cactus and the lights inside
the glass
infinite and infinitely
this night
back in my bed
trying to breathe so i can see the future
but it's just channel thirty-four
and barking dogs
and the phone
and her voice
and my life
and bare breasts at a window
and her life
and she is crying
and she is crying

i know that sound
and she is crying
and what do i feel
do you feel anything
she says
anything at all
and i put my right hand
inside my shorts
and think that it's already october
and what i feel
is only pain.

eternal uneventful things

it's been cold
the last couple of weeks,
but this morning
there is sunlight
and it comes through
the windows
as i pour a cup of hot water
and stick
a pear in my mouth,
laughing
because i remind myself
of a roasted pig,
an apple in my mouth
and the x's for eyes,
like when we drew them
as kids.

walking to my desk,
i stop at the living room
and
see my father
with his arms raised
the way
i used to
hold mine in the air,

wanting my cousin diane
to pick me up.
i take the pear
from my mouth,
the soft skin punctured
and wet
with spit,

as
he remains standing there
at the window,
washed in sunlight,
his eyes closed,
letting the heat take him
far enough back,
i imagine,
to the years
when there was more
than just this waiting
to die.
i move on,
leave him alone
to thaw
and uncurl his fingers
as he thinks of eating sardines.

i go to my desk
and sit for hours,

writing uneventful things
until the light
goes away.
the gate creaks
and my mother walks past
the window,
telling me that
it's not quite yet
time for him
to go.

i nod.
today,
the two of us,
father and son,
we
are
eternal.

pure

the pier
the cold wind
the blood and fish stained railings
rusted and sticky
standing
shaking and hungry
casting out my line
one more time
into the ocean
casting it with good intentions

the hook
the severed tail of an anchovy
the invisible line
arcing
into the air
caught by a draft
taken and dropped
away
far
from where i had wanted—
[twenty one years ago
and too small to look over
the rail
then made of wood

holding on to a gray fishing pole
with a missing eye
staring at the end of it
like my father tells me
waiting for it to twitch
and
mom is fishing next to me
with a 7-up can
line wrapped around the middle of it
her finger on the line like she is
checking for its pulse]

[and we pull up
the mackerels
and kingfish
and celebrate the blessing
there must be
over fifty fish spilling
out of the buckets
this is
the first time
i have ever been to a pier
the first time
i have seen life caught
then—]

[the night
years later
my father and i alone

wearing matching gray
los alamitos windbreakers
he has taken me
fishing
because he has something
he wants to tell me
but
he never does
we stand side by side
bent over
leaning against the rail
our elbows stained
with scales
without talking
trying to feel
the biting cold
on the skin of our hands]

and
these few seconds—
frozen
pure
once again here
in a dirty spot
seagulls snatching up
the cut bait
a small splash
from the darkness
beneath

and
i put my eyes
upon the black water
my eyes
upon the black water
my eyes
upon the things
that ask for me
to pull their lives
into mine

the mexican couple
next to me
is catching much more—
i am not good at this
i wish i knew
what it was that my father
had to say to me that day
when he chose
to remain silent
by my side
if it could have been
something about
the secret to fishing
or why the scales shine
in the dark
on the belly
of a fish
or

something about
giving birth to a life
that you watch
struggle
root
bloom
bear fruit
wither
and die.

breaking bread

we'd drunk too much wine
in the saturday afternoon sun
and when it got dark
and past midnight,
when everyone else had gone,
she followed me to my room
and we crawled into bed,
trying to be quiet
because only a thin wall
was between us
and my parents.

she asked me to get condoms
but i was too drunk to remember
about the ones i hid under the books.
we kissed,
swallowed each other's tongues,
rowed our boat
to canada
where we hung our hearts
on a lime tree,
gave our eyes
to the bulls,
placed them in their teeth,
cut off our fingers

to see who needed more,
and we whispered,
your skin smells so clean
your skin smells so clean.

and the morning this way—
laughing at the new sun,
at the shadows
made through the french windows,
this place we don't know
like contentment,
a sunday morning holiness;
the smell of butter from the kitchen
and my father sneezing
and hymnals on their radio
and the sound of newspaper pages flipping
and how we couldn't turn away
from the sheer curtains,
from the light outside,
and how we couldn't turn toward each other
because there was too little space
between us
for anything more—
the marks on our bodies,
the lipstick and dried cum,
traces of love confessed,
fading on her pale skin.

at the breakfast table
my father put his left hand
on my shoulder
and she began to cry
and mom looked at me
and i told her that she was too drunk
to drive home
and mom nodded
and i forked a pancake
and put it on my plate
and put pieces in my mouth
until i had an excuse
not to speak,
stuffed myself
until i had a reason
to be a coward,
as my father's hand slipped off
my shoulder
and mom told her she looked skinny
and next to me,
she continued to cry.

fabric

two weeks away from marriage.

i'm standing in front of the mirror
wearing nothing but her black panties
as if this is how i can carry her with me
while she is in charlotte
eating pulled pork
waving goodbye to her old swimming pool
to the girls in love with pale guys in glasses
to her pink room with the slanted ceiling.

when i was four
there was a vanity in my mother's room
and i found her bras
and i thought the cups were perfectly shaped
to cover my ass cheeks
and that day i started putting everything on my skin—
chocolate
silk
hands
blood
shit
corpses
prayers
dirt.

my body looks ridiculous like this
the bit of shiny fabric over my dick
making the rest of me look
undone
my flesh unfinished
i liked it much more darkened
on the streets of paraguay
shirtless and brown
feet bare
but all that is temporary
when we hold our curses dear until the end—

my yellow skin
the empty pages that never stop.

scarring

my face in the sun,
the rain returned to the graveyard,
finding the left arm of god
and the scar
where i lose my faith
in the last three words of grace.

to kneel,
without a name,
washing the feet of death
with cold dry lips,
because i don't know how to ask
for one more lifetime.

only cowards can write this poetry,
terrified that nothing
will remain of us,
footsteps washed in the storm,
a sneeze muted by bombs,
our skin forgotten in ovens.

outside there is shoveling of dirt
to plant roses,

unable to speak loud enough,
terrified of the scars that hide,
of the healing that finds,
of the words that leave.

one human gallery [self-portrait #4]

she laughs.
the coffee is lukewarm
in my hand,
in the paper cup that leaks
slow drops.
i rip off a piece
of the almond croissant.
it's too sweet.

we sit by the skinny tree
without a name,
its shade on the used up sidewalk
of a quaint neighborhood.
there is money
resting
in the cracks on the ground
made by high heels
and fat kids
and i reach over,
flick dust
from her yellow shirt
with the two green mantis praying,
causing her to stop
the laughter
for a second.

and we join hands,
drawing lines in the air,
helix and circus animals,
point reaching point,
lines tethered to pink stockings
and torn lips,
all for its simplicity
and the forest of alchemy,
and in the hot sun
i pull away,
wrap these swollen arms
around my torso,
trying to hold in the pigments
of my immediacy.

but she worries
that i will learn to embrace the uncalled blessings,
for what am i
but yellow parchment
stretched across the slender
spine of a kite in spring;
what am i
but 170 pounds of a present we can't name.

this is the moment
of shortening necks
and a busy phone at the family home
and her arms cutting through the air
as she teaches me

how to embrace the river,
how to swim in the flood of bile and brown spit,
how to stand on a slippery floor,
silent and calm,
while my father squats down,
opens the bottom drawer by the dining table with
a loud screech,
picking through a file,
three hammers,
crazy glue,
and a green pocket-sized gideon's bible
for a "d" battery
even as i tell him
that i will reach the end of our street
with steps taken
from hatred.

nothing is blind.
nothing in my life is blind.
these incisions are precise and well-intentioned.
this is the moment
of hanging the body of our work
on hooked branches
and snapped bones,
opening the word for the last time together,
finding god,
and how we are etched in stone
by the deeds we failed to prevent.
i am but sin and the people i have hated.

this yellow is the worthlessness of my ancestors.
i see nothing but the blood of your children
seeping into the gravel of my garden.

she reaches for my hand
as i lick the spilt coffee from my finger.
diane is moving to hawaii with her parents
and mom's teeth are hurting again
and all around us
they walk,
they breathe,
they manage smiles and courtesy
as we hang ourselves in the clean walls of
a well lit gallery
on opening night,
with portuguese cheese plates
and french champagne,
where people stand
with arms hooked around someone else's bent ones,
eyes furrowing over
the details
of our lives,
wondering about the blank background,
about the thin lines,
about the blunt red
strokes
dripping
down
over a clean white surface.

the sweetness

the details repeat each day—
the man on bronson off eighth street
combs his hair upstairs in his bathroom
before he walks out of the house,
waving at his fat wife,
who stands on the porch in her robe,
as he drives off
in his red thunderbird.

in here too—
closing myself off.
holding on to it
if it is pain,
until it becomes something
i can cherish.

the ants have come out in the kitchen,
crawling on the cutting board
and the two blue wine glasses in the sink.
i forgot to wash them this morning
after my ex came by
with two dozen donuts
to go with
my half bottle of stolen wine.

she started to cry
because the blue wine glasses
i found in the back of the shelf
were the ones we'd bought last year
during a home sale at macy's.
they were some of the details
we'd planted in our lives
to create a picture of a future together
that was more
than what we had.
and as she cried,
i poured two
and we drank it down.

i find them all around the house
like flowers planted in secret—
a candle holder wrapped
in white tissue paper
hidden under the clean underwear,
a set of six colored port glasses,
a silver picture frame,
pictures of the dogs
in different stages of growth
as if we were learning
to draw lines on doorways,
to document the growth
of the children we thought
we'd have.

her spare key.
her expired driver's license,
her hair still long
in that picture.

i inhaled the coconut scent
of the suntan oil on her arms
as her phone rang
and she talked to her new man.

the ants will soon smell the sugar
of the two boxes of donuts
on the coffee table.
i wait for them.
i wait for them to smell the lavender
on the chair where she rested
her jacket.
i wait for them
to smell the smoke
of her sunburned skin.
i wait for them to come out
to cover the boxes,
to cover everything,
to walk with so many small feet
all over the sweetness of
my life.

crying out for tragedy like all beautiful things

I.

in the mornings of a korean winter—
holding my breath while running out into the front yard,
the icicles hanging from the roof like bats
as mom yells after me,
waving the striped sweater in her right hand.

but i don't ever stop
and this time i don't fall,
i don't slip on the frozen steps and drop
on my ass,
because my brother is not there
to make me fall on the ice just by telling me
i would.

"he slips and he falls," he'd always say
and there i'd go,
again and again and again.

but not this time,
not this morning of white lights
and gray cracked walls
built by god [built by god built by father].

this morning of mouth wide open,
crying out for tragedy like all beautiful things,
and the way my feet melt the snow
when i am more frozen
than the sky.

II.

the silhouette of the dog hanging from the balcony—
i'm too short to reach up and touch its frozen tail.
i'm too short to reach up and touch death.
mom's voice soothes me,
telling me how all dogs die in winter,
and i count the links of the chain
of the leash that held it contained in its life,
my feet sinking through the melting of snow,
into the frozen wish of my brother knowing so much of me.

III.

if i should stay
i would only be in your way

and if i sing these words enough times,
until the neighbor across the street finishes chopping down
the cypresses he bought and planted in his yard

in which his scared child can hide from everything,
if i sing it enough,
just one more time—

goodbye please don't cry
we both know that i know what you need

i want to believe,
lying in the darkness under a rain stained ceiling,
that it's not her,
the one i killed before she felt one winter,
i will believe that this untouched voice
belongs to dolly parton
as i roll over, and away, on to my side.

IV.

we fight at the edge of the cliff,
the water breaking like frail bones of sparrows
against the teeth of the rocks below.
it wants the dim light i hold in my cupped hands.

i have seen this fight before—
on the side of a mountain between an angel and a young man
who didn't know any better,
who got away with a mere broken hip.

i hang on, hang on to what this is,
nails buried in the cement of westchester place,

in the black tar floor of my los angeles,
on the side of the mountain.

the angel wants my soul.
but where was he when i sat in the bathroom
of a santa barbara carrows,
a gun on my lap, praying for the strength to die?

it's too late.
he can't have it.
i have claimed all the dead of my life.
and i will claim
the living too.

the healing

i count in sequence the burgundy marks
on my body that she has left—
on my chest,
two on the right side where my muscle so often stops
functioning,
one more mark lower down closer to the heart
and centered,
right next to the cheloid.

at the medical center in downtown off waverly,
the nurse is excited because she lives in brooklyn too.

'what part?' she asks

'bushwick,' i say

'ooooohhhh,' she says

and she tells me she is afraid of men from bushwick,
her hand touching this place,
this scar from healing too much.

cheloid is a difficult word,
sounding like cracked roofs and birch leaves.
i'm trying to think of a way

to write that there are many parts of me
that have already died,
but it's impossible.
so i just stand here,
at the elevator pushing
the sideways pointing button,
and stare at the parts of me that's still visible
beneath all the places where the blood
has risen to the surface,
this body that breaks in uneven fractures,
pieces falling on the backyard
like bottlecaps and peppercorns.
i don't know how to heal right
so i beg her to scar me.

it is all too much today.
i am waiting for the weight of the scars
to shatter my bones,
to cut off my air like a soft blue pillow
but i can't say goodbye,
i just can't
because i need to love my last seconds,
love something right
just once.

taste of life

drinking til 3 a.m.,
then the subway.
walking from the station uphill,
one sleepless night moving into the next;
over an alcohol horizon
where i lose the measure of balance—
the sun beginning to rise,
the cold sharper in the light.

this morning i opened
my eyes, stared at the ceiling,
fumbled in my shorts
for a release.
it is hunger, i told myself,
it is hunger and nothing more,
this breaking below my ribs.

i have chased it to new york,
through broadway and christopher st.
st. marks and avenue b,
through the romance that betrays itself
each time my foot sticks
to spilt things
on the ground.

my hand shines with cum.
for a moment i think of licking it clean
to taste the possibility of life,
that which i fail each day
in holding.

secrets

if i could remember

how i took my first breath
it would all be easy.
but i. don't. won't.

the something before the scream.
the something before i cried.
the how things end.

gray mornings lately.
out at 6.45.
i get up drowsy.

the dogs on the porch
staring at the front door
long enough to open it.

each time—
hoping it gets easier.
hoping it doesn't.

outside
wet air holds skin.
he stared and

it happened again.
miracles—
door opening.

this is it.
the only time
walking together because

in the sun
we won't need each other.

in the sun
we will know what we're hiding.

in a few days, i'll be thirty one

my hands were
once beautiful.
i used to
thank god
for my hands
and for my eyes,
not the actual eyes
because
they are very small
and not beautiful
at all.
i mean,
my eyes,
like my eyesight.

i have just had
another breakdown
and
i look at
my hands tonight
after
i have finished
wiping away
all the stupid girlish crying
from my face

and gotten off
the carpet
with cracker crumbs
stuck on my back.

i was once
going to be a father.
she told me
about the pregnancy
in my car.
we were parked
somewhere in west l.a.
during her lunch break
and she told me
crying
as i chewed
on a hamburger
with my seat reclined.
and when we
decided
to get rid of it,
we were
standing outside
a small house near la cienega
and she pushed
my hand off her
and said,
you're not going to
stick around anyway,

and she walked
away from me.

it's weird.
we knew
the baby was going
to be a girl
and
i can't remember
the name
we had set on giving
our daughter.
it made us
so happy once to say
her name.
now i can't remember
it.

i am looking
at my hands
and they are still covered
in the blood
of the nameless
girl.
i thought
by now
i'd have washed them
completely.

in a few days,
i will be
thirty one years old.
i will be older
than my parents
ever imagined
their youngest son
to be.
my child would have been
four,
i think,
three or four.
she would have been
old enough
to talk to
and
she would have
sat on my chest,
laughing,
pulling at my beard
the way i used to
with my father,
on my chest
while i lay
on the carpet
with now blurry eyes,
telling myself
to breathe,
and i would have touched her

with my once beautiful
hands,
telling her
that i am old enough
now
to know
that you lose your life
one good thing
at a time.

white feathered wings

gathered around
the chopping block,
we waited,
hiding behind
our parents' legs,
peeking past their hips
and at each other,
at the rusted ax leaning
on the flat tree stump.
i heard them laugh
as the bird came fighting.
we moved out from behind the adults
as the man in the brown shirt
spit into his hands for show,
and while holding the bird down
with one big hand,
he lifted the ax up over his head
and brought it down.
when he let it go,
the head on the dirt
beneath the chopping block,
the chicken began leaping
into the air,
falling and leaping again,

flapping white feathered wings
all over the field,
the blood spraying from its neck
and planting red daisies
in the ground.
we ran.
we scattered,
grabbing parents that didn't
belong to us,
to bury our faces in their sides
until it stopped.
there was a fire large in the pit
and men drunk under the mango tree.
i ran away and sat on the bumper
of a brown station wagon,
trying to figure out
what my father had meant
in the car that morning
when he'd reached over
and tucked some loose hair
behind my ear
and had told me to say goodbye
to my friends because we were leaving
for america.
i'd been playing with the button
on the glove compartment
and the door had flipped open
when i'd pushed it too hard,
paper falling out on to my lap and floor.

i'd gone down to pick them up,
curling myself up under the dashboard.

you have to learn to be cold, he'd said then,
if you want to become a man.

he walked over to me
with a plate of food
and we bit the cooked meat
off the legs and the wings
and i started to cry
as i took another bite
and washed it down with coke.

good, huh? he said.

i nodded.

damsel

and

plastic

and blue

blanket

winters

thieves like us

we talked on the phone,
each of us watching
the bicycle thief
on pbs in our own dark rooms,
and she asked what was happening now
and i said that dad was beating
on my brother for losing his money
and she said that
this was a strange and sad movie
we were watching.

how we sleep

we like to leave the window open
and kick off the sheets,
forgetting how mom told me to always
keep my stomach covered.

we like to lie on the couch
and listen for the screams that arouse us
because i have grown up in los angeles
and all i know is violence.

last night we parked the car
and walked into the street.
a car sped toward us.
we were frozen as it swerved past.

we left the street and walked in
and once inside the apartment,
i put the pot
and the bag of canned vegetables

on the floor by the dog,
then we held each other,
crying
with the lights on.

blue skin of dead things

it is blue.
it is blue skies.
it is blue morning
through the window
waking me up.

the kids are playing outside,
games that don't exist,
like running into
each other
at full speed
in search of laughter.

there are t-shirts
and mini skirts,
bare arms
and bare legs.

i'm still
inside my room,
trying to find a space
on the floor
to place my bare feet.

the laundry and sheets of paper
have piled up
so much.

i have neglected to do the little things
and now there is no space for me
in here.

i go into the living room,
turn the tv on,
watch how the world ends.
turn it off again.

i am out of bread.
i am out of strength.
i am out of wanting.

it is blue.
it is blue disappointment.
it is blue skin
of dead things.

i have no more clean clothes
so i will
remain naked
because it is spring
and it is too late
for shame.

this is the dawn

i nudge her awake.
it's not even 6,
but i want her to see
this orange sun hanging
outside our window.

that's amazing, she says.

i keep waking her up.
a couple of hours ago
i woke her up when i heard
our downstairs neighbor moaning.

listen, i said,
someone else in this building's
getting fucked.

we're just lying here.
the alarm is still set
to go off in a little over an hour.
the orange sky and the orange sun
over brooklyn
becomes the point
where i can begin.
she has fallen back asleep.

her hand rests on my chest
for a few beats,
then she rolls over,
her back to me,
her back to the windows,
because her body remembers
that the light will be unbearable
when it comes.

i turn too
and look at her back
and remember those words
i lost in the skin of her neck
when i first leaned in
close enough
to smell the drying sweat.
i roll back over,
trying to imagine what
my lips
look like as
they move under the orange light,
then lie as still
as i can
on my back,
my eyes shut tight,
one finger of my left hand
hooking the elastic
of her panties,
and i wait

for the sounds of the living
below
to rise up
and fill us
again.

two eggs scrambled

i crack the last two eggs
into a bowl and whisk
while gould plays bach on the radio,
his breaths loud
like the blood that boils
in my arms.

a cockroach mulls over
a few day-old crumbs
in the sink.
i open the faucet
and add water to the eggs
to give it more volume.

i scramble the eggs,
put a piece in my mouth,
and toss the rest
in the trash,
walk the bottle of wine to the window,
choke on the warm air
that smells like the clean bones
of dead bulls.

in front of the laundromat
across the street,

a little girl is showing
her mom how to do a handstand,
her hands on the dirty sidewalk,
smooth young legs
and two pink slippers kicked in the air—
miracles upon miracles;

yelling,
"you're upside down, mom!
mom, the cars are parked in the sky!"

i slow down the drink
because when the wine is gone,
the girl will also be gone
and the lights will come on
on the triborough bridge
and an old woman with a limp
will get on the bus on amsterdam and 57th,
ask the driver if it will take her to 106th,
as i move away from this window
and crawl into bed,
close my eyes,
and dream of
nothing.

ghosts

twenty. twenty days here.
today we woke up at noon,
smelling like cigarettes.

i finally crawled out of bed
and went out to the living room naked,
pushing the red curtains aside
to stick my head out the window
and check on the clothes,
my white t-shirts and judy's underwear,
hanging on the clothesline.

mom used to hang-dry our clothes in korea
back in the early part of the seventies
before we left for south america—
all for me and my brother,
as my father used to remind us
whenever i left my books in the locker at john burroughs
because i didn't have homework.

"we came here for you two, for your education,
and you leave your books at school!"
dad would yell.

"well, dad, they have these things called lockers,"

i'd start to say
until he'd pick up the bat
and i'd shut the hell up.

anyway, mom used to hang-dry our clothes,
my diapers hanging like so many flags of surrender
across the living room during winter
so they wouldn't freeze.

there's a story they've been telling
about one particular night
when a burglar broke into our house.
i was just a baby then,
the story goes,
and at the peak of my diaper usage.
we were all asleep,
my father after another long day of construction work,
mom after another long day
of standing in the kitchen
over boiling pots and chopped cabbage,
of picking me up and putting me down.
the burglar got in the house,
the story continues,
and stepped into the dark living room,
searching for treasured things
in blindness, in silence,
until he, the burglar, found himself screaming,
nearly falling on the coal warmed floor backwards,
his face flushed as white as the apparitions

floating near the ceiling,
stretching from wall to wall,
screaming at the damp cloth squares
hanging still in the air,
"ghosts! ghosts!"
before running out of our house
into the winter night.

the air is getting cooler
at the square by the sant joan church,
an old building that gets lost
amongst the grandness all over barcelona.
the jug of cold red wine at lunch
that we had with rabbit a la brasa
and a perfect potato is making me sleepy.
i impressed judy with my spanish skills.
i tell her i have found myself using words
that i never realized i knew.
it's about getting my skin and bones out of the way.

my parents haven't told the diaper story in a long time.
maybe i'll bring it up when we get back
and see them again.
still 2 months to go in this healing time.
maybe i'll even ask them how they knew if they were asleep
what the burglar saw
and what he was screaming at,
how they know so many details
that passed through our house
as we slept.

embers

we rub our eyes at the light
and spit too close to our scuffed shoes.
we don't know what to do with our hands,
careful about everything that breathes
when we can't see.

we push out our chests and fill ourselves
with the burning and smile.
it's easier to greet each other
over common disasters,
telling small lies about the love we seek.

an old man kneels on the sidewalk,
bowing to a half of a brick slammed down
on day old noodles and rice puked drunk,
saying he'd like a roof too
so he could duck his answered prayers.

an ash falls on my wife's nose.
it looks like it's waiting for something.
i reach out and flick it off with my finger,
then watch my skin begin to disappear
beneath all the ash, all the remains of burnt things.

it's getting closer. i smell it in the smoke now—
that love letter my father wrote hunched over

against the wall with a turned back and dirty nails,
until his life became too embarrassing
to share with his children.

the man gets up.
this morning, covered in ash,
we are becoming colorless,
remembering how thirsty we are as we breathe the smoke,
learning in the fire
to pray for a cup of water.

because i could not stop for death

today i love emily dickinson
because her rhymes make less sense than her pain.
i am in my cocoon of dirt and pulled weed,
father's sweat and yarn dog chewed into joy,
holding seven dollars in my fist
like fireflies over japanese graves.

msg and month old pork
work at my stomach
as i watch him dig up the yard outside,
hunched over,
the way he used to look down on me
as i lay by mom on the floor
waiting for him to come home,
drunk, a bag of pastries in his hand,
asking me if the ghosts came back today,
if the ghosts came back
in that house made of gray stones,
three floors of promise,
a balcony of dead dogs
and the jars of chili paste molding in the yard.

mom asks what i want for dinner
and i nod to everything she says
because she doesn't whisper,

she doesn't whisper anymore
and my legs have started hurting again,
my spine too,
how the doctor says my spine is weak
and that's what numbs my legs.
it got bad in new york,
trying to walk down second avenue
to the bar on saint marks
with my knee locking up every third step.

the chinaman gave me deer antler juice
to drink twice a day
and he studied my name
and the way i talked and said hello
and he says he wants to teach me
everything he knows
because he knows that i was supposed to be a healer,
not knowing about the day i went to the hospital
to see my grandfather,
the one that wanted me to go kill myself
to save the family from my disgraceful life.
i went to temple hospital
because he'd been in my dream,
in the back of a bus,
waving through the window at me
as the smoke from the exhaust made everything invisible.
i stood by his bed,
shuffling my pair of black nike air force,
staring out the window

at the exterminator building,
and when he closed his eyes
clutching the rail with his right hand,
i held my own right hand over his chest
and prayed—
god, here i am, use me, make him well.

and i believed because there is a frame
that mom hangs by my desk no matter
how many times we move,
a quote from first samuel—
you will do great things and find victory.
i believed as i stood again next to his bed
a month later,
this time watching my mother
as she stared at that same chest,
saying he can't be dead because it's still moving.
it's still moving.

we are outside feeding the dogs.
chico finishes and lays down,
licking himself like a cat.
my wife is training our new puppy to sit,
to down, to roll over,
but the puppy now only rolls one way.
she is trying to get the pup to go the other way.
she is pushing the dog,
trying to flip it over,
and i pull my hood over my head

and bury my hands in my pockets
as she falls back on her ass and laughs—
bella!—laughing—come on, bella!—

and i ask the chinaman
if he can teach me
how to save myself,
because my wife is on her ass,
laughing,
as bella tries to
sit,
down,
paw,
roll,
all at the same time,
while i stand still,
wanting to hold on to this moment,
not wanting it to ever
come to an end.

riptide

they stand at the water,
the women,
where the foam divides
the sand from the ocean,
the water that seems endless
behind them,
their bodies caught like fish
in bathing suits too tight.

the women stand at the water
with their toes splitting apart
and sinking
into the sand,
their daughters deeper in the water,
with skin brown and sweet
in the sun.

and i stand under the umbrella
with my stomach falling out
of the red swim trunks
that hang off my smooth young hips,
and they point at me,
wave for me to come to them,
to feel the cold water,
to cleanse the tops of my feet.

i put my right hand over my eyes
to shade away the light
and smell the coconut in the air
as the couple next to me,
beautiful and happy,
rub each other with oil.

they call to me–

come come
drink from the well
bow your head under the blood
falling
falling
the shell of an elephant
made of sulfur
like the cross born under the bed
and curses folded
like nightgowns in the closet
come come
drink from the well
drink from the sand
drink from the springs
of a fucking mess.

i shake my head
and pull up my shorts
on the left side,

rub my stomach.
they laugh
and keep calling to me.

maggie,
skinny and freckled,
walks out of the water
from behind them,
pulls back her wet hair until
it all disappears behind her
and i look at her breasts
already growing full
into a woman's figure
and the blue fabric of her swimsuit
wedging into her crotch,
and i am afraid to open my mouth
afraid to burn my tongue
afraid to burn
the unsaid words
afraid to burn inside.

i feel my body rise up
into the air,
held up like a sacrifice
as i spread my arms,
letting them fall toward the ground
as i push my chest up,
breaking my heart through my bones,
my legs bent and limp

at the knees,
my father's big hands holding me
as if i am
just born.

i am isaac.
i am the lamb
caught in the bush.
his voice is comforting
beneath me
as he takes me to the ocean.

come come
swim in the sky
rip the flesh
to find your skin

come come
ghost of mary
dance on the brown of
a dying field

and i drink another glass
of old scotch
and fall asleep on the couch,
a body twitching on my shoulder,
waking up with my hand
on her cheek
as peace comes to me

like cold foam on my feet
like the sun on my eyelids
like fingers curling
at my chest.

fake like love

mom rubs her sock-covered
feet against each other
like a cricket
and my father is there too,
his stomach turning audibly
with some virus,
under the dim ceiling lamp
that is missing the three bulbs
that were removed
to save money on electricity.

faith is difficult
and fake like love
as she covers her small mouth with
her plump fingered hand
and she yawns
and i push into the black couch,
not knowing how,
not knowing how this
or that,
how to string the words together
to say
that love is
a broken windshield of winter mornings

or just that i don't think we are
going to survive.

i have been thinking of a word
that i never use because
it sounds uncomfortable.
in my head,
i am repeating the word
precarious,
knowing that
i will never use that word again
in anything that i write.

i look out the window
waiting for the rain that
stopped off briefly
this morning
as i turned the corner
on third street
and headed home.
but it is still too dark
and gray
and the patch of grass in the backyard
is yellowed and dry.

it is difficult to find
anything in days like this:
a broken pencil in a pile of leaves

the left brown slipper bought for two dollars
some other things i can't think of
a hand dangling from the branch holding a ribbon
my head falling upside down from the book
enough anger to give me a reason to get up
tomorrow sprouting under the lime tree.

my father curses
the empty liquor bottles on my floor
and his own loud stomach,
unaware of his uncle that will die first thing
in the morning in brazil.
my eyes are on the floor
by my feet
and i see that my toenails have grown
and that i have failed
to take care of them
for too long.

karaoke

the empty plastic bottles,
kirkland brand from costco,
pile up on top of the desk
next to a bottle of bushmills
next to a bottle of sake,
two cameras pointing at me and a skinny wallet.
the drier still smells like fish from the towels
mom used the other night cutting up
the fish mr. lee caught on a boat
and brought over on sunday.

when i came home sunday afternoon,
i found my dad on the couch with mr. lee,
a microphone in his hand,
words wiping yellow on the big screen
my brother bought for him,
over pretty pictures of clouds and orchids.
i stopped just inside the door,
quiet, lifting my right foot up
and trying to take off my shoe
and i listened to him sing three more words
as a flock of birds flew low
above the water that reflected their flight.

when i breathed too loud,
he turned around
and we looked at each other,
not knowing what to say,
as has been for so long,
this dumb,
this stupid,
this mute between us,
him on the couch
while i try to stand
on one leg
without breathing.

the mountain in an-yang

the sun goes down—
this blue gate that opens to night, the footsteps and wheels
that crush the new grass pushing out of fresh laid dirt.
i have heard these sounds before
and remember how we gave them names
like winter, like summer, like black, like wind.

we're a convoy of the dead going up the mountain
in an-yang to visit grandfather and grandmother, side by side once more.
they never expected me. i've been gone so long
and gone again soon enough. the others sit in a circle
and wail their sorrow and others still comb
the twin mounds of soil for weed.
my father wipes the bricks that frame the graves
with a wet rag and a bucket of water,
finding a worm at the edge, which he picks with anger
and tosses down the hill that leans like god in thought;
the slope that tilts the horizon to that point so far
below us where we hang and dry agony and wet shirts.

i put my finger on my name on this page, pause for each letter.
i have become the shepherd of my name.
if one letter was to get lost, i would
search for it day and night, climbing
rocks torn and creased up to the mountain,

our mountain, again, alone, wine spilling
from the bottle in my right hand, kneeling down
under the cloud, wiping the headstone stained by winter
until i find my name engraved,
third from the right just as i found it for the first time
as my father picked worms, cold and silent,
waiting to be called to life,
waiting to fall to the ground.

tides

white boy joel called our neighborhood a ghetto
and swam in his pool hidden behind tall walls
splashing water loud enough for us to hear.

when he stepped out on his lawn
rubbing his belly under his t-shirt
we shot him in the face with a bb gun and
ran away as blood flowed out
six seven inches in front of him
spraying the green grass.

we went to see's candies
on the corner of wilshire and oxford
to see alice in her see's candies uniform
but she wasn't there.

the other girl working kept crying
telling us that alice wouldn't be back for a while
and she gave us some coffee and butterscotch
suckers when we left.

at home
my father chased me around the apartment
with a bat that night yelling,

you want to kill somebody?
i'll show you how to kill somebody!

i lost him around the couch
and ran out the back door
and sat on nick's porch
where dogface cassie told us
alice was raped by five friends on the beach.
we smoked another joint and went home.

and one day
i told my father i was leaving
and he sat up in his bed and cried
and we wrapped clumsy arms around each other
like two boys in love
but it was too late or too soon
for such things

and outside
the world
the sun
it shone upon me
it shone upon me
the sun
it shone upon me

and somebody walking by
kicked me on the head
to wake me up on a san pedro sidewalk

empty bag of fries in my hand.
i went down to the beach
and watched the wave roll in and out
the foam dissolving
the water shining under the sun.

my feet sank in the sand
thinking of my first grunion run
how we pulled them out of the wet ground
stealing time before the water returned
until there was nothing left but holes
that would also disappear

and i knew
somewhere in front of my eyes
there was supposed to be beauty
the small flawless things that hold god
but i couldn't see them
they had left with the tides
with promises to return.

i walked down the beach
the water swaying to my right.
i kept walking
toward home
to wake my father once more
to ask him
to show me
how to die.

this writing about the terror

my footsteps
falling through cracks
gaping on this porch made of bondo
and loose leaves with no symmetry,
chicken-scratches on god's prison wall
counting off days of our thirty-eighth year,
counting to alpha,
counting to jerusalem,
counting to my third finger dotted with blue ink.
they lie, they lie on the evidence
of my misguided journey—
a dead roach, mosquitoes just landed,
robert,
the three dogs,
wife,
our baby unborn,
dad [calling him dad here],
a snail,
that tiny woman [no longer petite,
with a knack for crochet whom i know as mother].
there are others too off on the side,
on the poison oak
and other shrubbery too particular to be identified,
lovers not so fresh dead
that i have started calling them carcasses.

i am from that country on the cold gray
step down into the kitchen where
mother stood with her back
curved out toward me. i leave
them there because i can only hate
the living and to touch them would
mean i would die. i leave them
there because my fingers can't
hold more than sticky keyboards, stuck
between a and s, between y and u, between
x and childhood fantasies of rape, between
the comma and regretting, between one
letter and the next and all the ones that brick
nonsense and shame.

the open blinds.
a smile in frames.
damsel and plastic and blue blanket winters.
my bleeding stomach.
my father trapped in my spine.
acupuncture will save him.
or at least let him breathe inside my posture.
eden lies to me.
i will eat the apple this time.
her beauty.
the black arrow of new best
before the complete text of mourning.
electra electra and
wearing a striped tie across the brooklyn bridge.

we took pictures of the water
and our minutes of joy,
and there was no chance for tired feet
or turning back
because patsy grimaldi waited under
the bridge, on the other side,
on the other side, on the other side of failure.

i am back and not alone, this hand
on my right shoulder,
the upside down when i tilt my head back,
backlight making her shadow,
like that dream of hell when mother shook me
awake on gramercy drive,
the last time i heard my name.
the last i heard it.

god is taking away my hearing
as i shuffle these numbed feet
once more west on the sparkles
of a west hollywood boulevard,
through a tuesday night silence,
past two boys with clean hair,
past corpses of divinity
and decent words uttered,
past schubert and beatles in the back room
of my baby's carcass
past yellow teeth shaman riptides of santa monica
and virgin mary past this ocean i once skipped

with one gleeful bounce
past my father's house frozen in the hands
of my ghost past god's words scribbled
by grandma while she lay on her left side
waiting to die past my skin past my name
past my sins past washington square
and the girl bleeding in the fountain
past nuyorican and the lies of the poets
past that fenced place in downtown
that is no longer a place past the past
past black fences past brown grass
past dug holes past this moment of panic
when i am terrified to know the next
and the last.

still life

the travel goes beyond black fences and landmines
of family secrets. the wings bought to take
me over the clouds and the rubber plants long
dead inside their skin made of hope.

i'm searching, you see, the rocks from my childhood
under dark brown staircases, the rocks shaped
like friends in ecuador who knew of summer heat.
those rocks i saw with the eyes carved out with
old knives stained with mackerel and lime,
searching, searching for memories that grown
men can only think they remember.

oh, it was brief, sometime this morning, but there
was pink in the sky by the yellow/green flags
flapping on the roof of a new apartment complex.
it was gone before i could understand, because
the stories of my childhood, the ones i heard
under silk blankets embellished by hand-stitched
cranes, were not told in colors, but with a finger
to the lips, my feet pulled out into the open,
a few careful moments of silence, and a smile.

when will i cry again? who has left me on the
other side of the land of hurricanes? another

glass of wine! as if i can pour enough new blood
into me to force out the death that flows through
these veins.

but this is still life. this desk of brown wood
sanded and varnished in june while the dog bled
from its ears, the drop of water on the wood
losing itself, taking on the color of its surface.
it will soon lose everything to the world to
conquer it.

so much space

but what clutter!—the pink bucket softened with
an old t-shirt to catch the rain in silence—the ceiling
plaster peeling and a hole punched with a red handled
screwdriver to drain the trapped water pouring
down so red—like pomegranates on the small tree
by which i peel off piss soiled pants for mom,
on one leg, balancing my weight on her left shoulder
with my hand—it's funny—as unexplainable, you know,
this ceiling—how such things that never lived can be
dying above me.

this was once the room where i stood naked
trying to make myself whole—the floor trembling
from the unbalanced washing machine—seeing
myself in the mirror just there—the way it trembles
again now—but there is only a television unplugged
and two speakers disconnected—the bucket too—the one
that catches—and so much space far from filled
by my lack—what i feel against the hardened
skin of my feet's bottoms is Li Po's breath
so still and broken—and the best way i know
to ignore her is to touch her spine that will
never heal—a week and a half and already leaving
us to wonder where god begins.

and this sound inside the hollow room is my wife
crying on my folded body—one hand from each of us
buried in the dog's fur—our hands find each other in
this place we cannot see——for once
it's not the dying that continues to destroy us
but our inability to forget that once we held
something that didn't so much mind being alive—
and i turn to my wife ready—finding
the perfect wet and muddy spot in the once crowded
back yard—and dig a small hole that can hold
this life we carry that once required so much space.

inexplicable walls—uncooperative roses

—the black out—the sirens—air cracking with each rushed
inhale—this is the waiting—crossed legs and hard concrete
steps—skin punctured on crooked nails pounded into
stained planks halfway—rusted heads stuck out like
the dull backs of whales in this placid ocean—for what
for what what—the armageddon—only the unreachable
punishment meant to cleanse the simple deeds of our regret
—counting the flies around the dog's bloodied numb ears—
black and red in the standing cling of the too long day—
unable to cut off the lost pieces of his body that can
no longer give him pain—the flies the flies—wings charged
with lightning tapping red rivers inside dead continents—
they have filled too many barrels with the weight
of the living—and the storm that finally comes—
unprepared—droughts more important than needing—they
fly away or imagined to be so quick to disappear

—he no longer bangs into new interruptions—inexplicable
walls—the calls he tries to catch with broken ears—choosing
still stoic and quiet in the rain that falls from the one
direction that he hasn't tried—tail sinking in such paced
measures—not unlike my father burying fish guts around his
uncooperative roses—the water rising in the grass of his
feet—drowned marks of his life in light—he chooses still—
he chooses to sink into the ocean he never imagined he could

touch—look dad—look—i am no longer afraid to swim—or
is that just the crushing of my teeth inside this mouth
too tight for repenting—stoic quiet in the storm unaware
that the tremors on his haunches rising through the knots
of neglected fur give him away—howling what he remembers
to be the sound of his sister's name

—as i hide my hands in the water—but i am found i am found
again—in this shelter of black disaster i have clutched—
and painted my face with bare knuckle punches until i was
more transparent than american black—i am found in the storm
that won't give me reprieve from the calling—the calling i
follow into the water—squat and ready—he takes enough
steps to bury his head in my legs—praying to god my hands
are strong enough to squeeze him to eden—promise promise me
or is it just the thunder—yes—night stagger and great
burnings—it is gentle to kill in misery—i promise
regardless having misheard prayers before—that it will be
still it will be silent it will be cold tiles and scents we
will never forget—and the hair on my leg moving then still
against the wind against the last exhale of his nose

—against this fan hung centered on white ceiling spinning—
drunk wilderbeast—and his ghost his scabbed ghost swaying
blind and sweet above our naked bodies—my wife dear wife
sleeping in a pillow of angry mothers and misdirected
fingers igniting more than this mount of dead dragons—
shielding her crying soul that was once saved with a skinny
raised hand—with a turned body—with the expanse

of her back that knows no broken lines—knowing knowing—
isn't knowing more than we were ever meant to handle—dragging
my nails over her skin waiting waiting for the storm of the blind

—as i get off the bed trying not to fall—seeing my leg
beneath that i can no longer feel—the slowness of buckling
into one's own burial—the sad fragment of some truncated
wish—i know it is so—loving myself for the first time
—the scar under my ring of gold—shedding blood again
on the page—to pretend that it is just my words that are dying.

the names we call

this porch, the dead leaves, and the crows come down
into my november, picking at the pavement of our street
where the sun no longer can. across the street,
the dog with one ear sleeps on the stoop, eight white
homemade ghosts and a dirty flag flapping above him

to his right, a tombstone buried in jest. the moon.
they say the moon bled two weeks ago, but i missed it.
tonight, we are the only ones left silent, this porch
of early november, four days from sixty two years since
the sudden appearance of one of the brightest and shortest gone

by the end of the month. the open hands letting me go, caught
by my own lacking moon, curved like those fingers that once
picked apples from a neighbor's tree, one by one, until
they curled around a pistol, an oar, a flag, the dark
obscuration of dust and matter, this spiral galaxy around us

showing. not being sure of freedom on a san pedro
sidewalk, but how could i have pushed myself up and
walked toward the water that morning of gulls and
french fries if i wasn't convinced it was my final chance?
the dogs behind black fences scream until

they lose focus, and the women weep when the cold hangs in
the dark. but we are not touched. our silence breaks
the chill to tempt us to endure. let forgiving be enough
and hearing his laceless black shoe shift on the dust
at the front door, his shoulder against the doorframe holding

up the weight of this yellow house, the breath leaving his body,
interrupted when he pushes the plastic teeth back into place
with his tongue. this was always the plan for the day's ending.
there on the grass hill the shepherd leaned a moment to look up,
asking the stars to accept his company, and to pass the time

he named them, made families. he saw beasts and angels. aiming
our gaze then too, as the day nears again, shifting our sights
from north to northeast of zeta, we search for the names we
will call each other. it is here. and he calls me. and i call
him, father.

indentation

the couch no longer holds my indentation.
the leather doesn't recognize me.
there are still two marks.
one belongs to my father and another one to mom.
hers is bigger because she stretches out
her small body to rest.
my father, he is usually sitting.
his eyes are shut.
his mouth is open as he starts to snore.

korean los angeles to greek new york,
queens to bushwick,
and back here again,
so many thousand miles and 19 boxes of books,
not counting the autographed selby hardcovers
that slipped out of a busted box and got lost,
all my movements tracked
by the surface of the couch.

i smell the fish soup,
the unwashed dog on the porch,
count jesus on all the walls,
the cross i made with popsicle sticks
and taped to the wall here above her head

as i fuck her ass, keeping quiet
so jesus and mom won't hear.

it is august.
the other night i opened the mail
to find my diploma that says i have now learned enough
and george rubbed at his large dry knuckles
while making last preparations
to open his first restaurant
and we looked at each other in the back yard,
the dogs nipping at our legs,
and i can't tell you what he was thinking,
but i wondered how long it has been since
i last fired a gun,
how many months or hours since
we drove through downtown,
george driving the van, me in the back
with the glock in my hand,
the plastic indenting the surface of my palm,
and how many years it has taken for us
to change the shape of the marks
that we etched into our skin.

speak

to

god

in

accents

the flood

the ceiling still hangs over me
like that,
white and knowing.
i pull my left arm out from under her pillow
and walk naked to the window,
stepping over the sleeping dog on my way.

i put my hands on either side of the glass
and lean forward
toward the deafening noise of the air conditioner
above the building next door,
the smell of spilt guiness
rising from the remains of a usc party
down below the sidewalk
at casey's.

and for a moment
a noise drowns out the motor outside—
my teeth grinding against each other.

i look out into the dark,
my neck stiffening up,
and hold my breath:

it comes now. it comes.

the first time i spent the night at her place
in brooklyn
i told her how i couldn't sleep
how i hadn't slept in more than 3 years
because of the nightmares
the visions of hell
of all the dead watching me run
through the dried field of wheat
and she told me that i was now protected
as the tiny fan at her window
the one with the ledge still specked
with dust from the trade center
across the water
cooled the sweat on our skin.

we are far from there tonight
and it has been so long
and like with all things
she keeps this promise
each night i scream for her in my sleep
but looking over my shoulder at her
her left leg bending out from beneath
the blanket stained with paw prints
i do not want her to see
how nights come
to such ends.

because the nightmares don't wait
until my eyes are closed—

this cold from the tiles rising
into my feet, into the bones,
into the architecture of my legs
of atrophy and brittle—

in this blue light of night
that dissolves the bruises on my skin
into restless irrelevance.
each night, i ask her to bite me
to cover my chest and stomach
with purple and black bruises
like stains of love and need,
counting up toward enough
that i no longer have to see myself,
to cover my skin entirely
so i can start from scratch.
the tones disappear now
in the darkened room.

the glass is cold against my stomach.
i look down and place my hand on the growing mound.
it reminds me of him and his father,
one that i remember, hovering above
as he lay on the floor after fish dinner
while mom cleaned up the dishes
and folded the table away,
lifting me up by the bottom of his feet
pushed up against my belly
as i screamed for him to not let my hands go

both of us laughing as my brother
waited his turn
and he let go as i held my breath
so i could learn to fly.

i go back to bed,
slip under the blanket until
my left elbow touches her burning skin
haunted by everything and father.

the ceiling,
holds no stars
no stars above los angeles
no stars above
the lines
the shadows
the dust
fingerprints by the hanging lamp,
i am here
like the shepherd at rest
who named the universe
to chase his loneliness
trying to find the planets on my ceiling
that i can call family

this poem is about my wife.
this poem is about my father.
this poem is about the universe.

this poem is about me.
this poem is about this sleepless night.
this poem is about how some things are eternal—

because she is breathing next to me
as i bury my fingers into my chest
between the marks she left this morning.

it comes now
the flood.
through downtown streets.
up the walls of our fortress.
through the cold windows.
across the cold tile floors.
into my feet, into the bones.
it comes
it comes now
and sleep is impossible because
it's all going to hell.

but i had held the sea inside me
so i wouldn't have to learn to swim
because it is too much
to practice survival.
so
let us laugh
as it comes,
this flood without focus,

only to move where there isn't
where there isn't
where there isn't.

it will not bruise.
my nails will puncture before i can bruise.
i will bleed when i want to be covered
in damages that can render
me invisible.

i turn my head
and bite her shoulder,
not heavy enough to wake her,
as i bury my fingers
as i bury my secrets under the melting
asphalt
of my summer skin
and in the mornings
          amen amen
            he teaches me to say—
wake up scratching
at the places i cannot reach,
where
i ignite and burn,
set the mountains of pusan on fire
because the only way
to calm the flame
is to shed the body i wear with so much
shame.

and in the darkness,
leaving—

      this poem is about the past 8 years
                this poem is about the way i lose
        this poem is about the ground that changes
                   this poem is about the snow
                   on the edge of los angeles
this poem is about a porch—

and i am the street
because i am nothing else
i am the corner of western and venice
soaking up the blood
flowing
from a small cracked skull
and this is the stain
that i kiss
this like all the others
is the stain
i push my tongue against
to remember how to wait
to remember how to scream
to remember that in 1985
a man fell off his motorcycle
and broke his head against the curb
as we waited with empty buckets
and bent poles
for the bus to take us to the fish in the ocean

to remember
that i don't care about the man at all.

it comes now,
the tanks,
over long neglected rooftops
and handshakes lost in
mid-curse.

to taste the hours
that slip through my lips,
i release her
from my teeth

the curve
of her shoulder
that carries
our vows.

there is too much
weight in it
and bones only remember
what breaks them.

these fingers
these nails
raking across and through my sternum
        after i break skin
                after i break through the surface   amen

of my enormity
dripping blood with each step
to make a track
to trace myself back
to my father
again
to grandfather's cancer
to grandmother's faith
to the complete
irrelevance of our failures
and
the meekness of our regret.

buried here
i'm buried
in fragments and skeletons
in brokedown pavements of war
in memories
                          lost at sea
of gestures i can no longer identify
on a porch
morning light
still air
       two bears and a dragon
              wanting to learn to measure in parallax
a rustling of shoes

in pieces
the verses of childhood

                    amen amen
fear eternity before the sin
i hear him say
his rough knuckled hand
gripping the bible
while i run in the street
on gramercy drive
closed off at both ends with orange cones
stolen from a bus accident

that the football made of sponge is tossed
four yards too strong,
landing on the windshield
of a beige buick century,
returning back up
into the air after the most silent bounce,
no longer remembered past the moment,
found again
tonight.

and in the sky,
in the light,
the birds gathered side by side
on the black wires like third grade boys
at lunch in the cafeteria.

the fourth one from the north end of the wire flaps
its wing first,
the first movement that causes the unrest,

how they all leap off the wire
to forget the disturbance,
the noise of flight caught in the blue air above.
the fourth bird,
the one with the brown spots
on its mostly white feathers.

but it isn't the wing,
          [this poem is not about the wing]
the first flap,
the bird with the missing left foot balancing without a word,
but the screen door
of 861 gramercy drive clanging back
shut behind evelyn,
her brown hands adjusting her
long and shiny ponytail.

she slides her flip-flops across the street,
the jean shorts pushed up so tight against her buttocks,
toward her little brother
who is still slapping his hands together
to lose the slippery dust from his palms
after the errant throw,
to rest her hand on his slumped
shoulder and say—
                something

in the bright july sky.   [or the one in november   not yet]
the birds give themselves away

to be mere pigeons,
each one holding its pair of wings
in the shape of a V,
a swarm of V's gliding uneasy,
no hawks or prairie falcons among them.

              she shifts next to me
                     curling her knees up as she turns toward
                     the window

as evelyn pulls her dark elbow away
when henry tickles it with a dirty finger,
running toward the football
still on the street from the incomplete pass,
in a puddle of car wash water by the gutter
and as so many fingers point
to the clouds beyond the pigeons,
at a dark solitary bird gliding down toward the earth,
the boy picks up the ball,
heavy now from all that
 it has soaked up from the pavement.

it comes now
and the fingers pick at the well worn chest
and i imagine i could have really used this life
to become somebody else—

an overweight girl
in new jersey getting pregnant
on her mother's bed with a boy who is too scared

or a man determined enough
to stand at the gate
without an umbrella
in a white shirt
and pockets full of bluebirds
waiting for the wine to pour
from the veins in the sky

joni mitchell singing
the regrets etched in her arms
like christmas songs
between the *i love you*
and the *i'm no longer here*

to become a dead leaf
shaped like a dying star
                              named by a shepherd at rest
brown and unforgiven
upside down caught at the ends of a burgundy string
tied to two green bubbles
holding thoughts in this comic book
that ends at volume one

where the balcony holds
more than
pale hands and dirty brushes
and names scratched out with popsicle sticks
and the paint drying in january
to be remembered by someone other than

to become
to fly out tonight on dusty wings
salvaged from a mid-winter divorce
with only a blue pen and a gray shirt
kiss the white spiders goodbye
and hang the windchimes on the lime tree
low enough for my past to reach
and a piece of green yarn
stolen from mom's basket
tucked inside my wallet

to stand outside the closed door
of a sunday morning
with my ear pressed to the wood
wet and cold
until i hear one ordinary word
dropped from her lips and lost
in the voice of the man who has spent
the night inside

my body is forgetting
in this dark room
how to be born on a used canvas
stretched out on the floor
at the foot of the bed
like poison under japanese footsteps
and yellow and white burnt sienna swimming
on my tongue
a rose taller than me

asking me who i am
the burning pot on the stove that remembers
things of getting old
and counting wrinkles
and in the middle of may
reaching out a tired hand to grab another
that shakes and

it seems
those nights in the living room
on gramercy drive
at the dining table with a typer
watching the clock
the hands shifting one minute at a time
hearing his snores coming down the steps
my heart in a fist
bracing itself for his voice
happened
so long
ago

and someday
someday
of the things
i remember
they will be filled with regret

                  cancer moon wanting
          cheap like red done wrong

like california
like the letter from
and about

no piece of paper
and sixhundredfifty
and five days in may

just a little
like seeing a little
a few drops left
and my tongue

drunken anchor
on her ring

such a neat tie
and i could tell you that i've seen

and living at the speed of light
and bubble gum
it disappoints us without warning
somewhere over fifty that way
and another so and so this way
and this is
like
the sun
shifting beneath my feet
finds the shame of the downstairs bed

and we burn ourselves
for a little light that lasts half a day
and the flesh
and the blood
and dying on the peaceful balcony

art thou not mighty?

                   and to see
                   it is no longer here

art thou not mighty, o youth?

            y la piedra
              su sangre
              cantan
           of ghosts and grace

of the things
i remember
they will be filled—

are you awake?
she turns,
her arm placed across my chest
as i slide my left arm back under her neck,

and before i answer,
she is gone again,
but i still say it,

tell her
that i am sifting through the words that i have read,
a lifetime of foreign objects,
the pages browning inside the cracked covers of little women
while waiting for him on the stoop.

even if
it is him,
it is he that haunts me from the pulpit
as i learned to sit on a pew
in a south american jungle,
trembling as a woman ran in screaming
words of satan, he says,
flinging herself face down
on the aisle,
her arms spread out like—

telling her
that it is this—
to ever want
for the smell
of my flesh
to be
a 6:30 a.m. poem
enough
to awaken her
in the morning

                                  selah

(i'll take nothing
i'll take nothing
i'll take nothing
but your fingertips
on my face...)

on that day
they sing this song

that is too far
that is too long
that is too far to visit the dead

1976   6822

la luna negra
laughing
her arms up
mujer maravilla
and the naked
books
stacks and stacks

for my love
that i can't control

a song
a psalm

on that day
they sing

turn your ear to my cry

oh you gates
oh ancient doors

it is him
my face up close to the window
shielding my eyes with my hands
to look inside
see clear into the kitchen—
my father is still grinding the beans
he needs to control his sugar level

the meteor shower outside
which i can not bear to watch
the courage it takes
to accept such a beautiful tragedy
does not exist
in me

on that day
they sing this song

our soiled forms
wrapped around
once snow covered
hills

on that day
they sing this song

promises scratched
on bare thighs
with unmanicured nails

3240   15 degrees
6123   and the summer

the hunters

the sudden
and waiting
to be in love
with everything

with everything -

jesus!
i am trembling –

this is the first commandment
and the second
like it
is this

twice in my lifetime
i have measured such windows

once while september reversed into the corpses of pigeons
and the other
when the smoke swallowed the world
and finding two old fingerprints smudged on the glass
one bigger than the other
belonging to different lovers.
i put my left hand on the first pane
and leave myself behind
as the steam lifts naked bones of goodbye arms
hanging like mistletoes from doorways
too narrow for words to pass through
it is no longer here
my love
it is no longer here

nor of the will of man properly deemed

and again i read here

of ghosts and grace

                                                    is the sun
                                                    is today

                            desnuda
                            she kept her scar below her rib
                            to be licked

the steps of things—
        abraham to isaac to jacob
        to judah to perez to zerah

and i
and i
turning to nectar
and they will catch my feet
bronze fingered demons
when i hold complete thoughts
to own myself larger
when after the bell buries
my daughter
in the mountains too high
for remembering
they will catch me
when i give birth to jellyfish
with my hands
because the stomach is filled
with next mistakes
next july
next everyone
        and the past november

i am lightning between small steps
and the line across
this face
so little belongs
make me the tattered end

of the lie that burns
make me sway on a concrete bridge
when the angels
careen forth infinitely shortcoming
i am lightning between
broken cigarettes
and chipped tooth kisses
before the ants crawl on fresh
resentments
and jesus trains with kendo sticks

boil the water
boil the ocean
boil tears that fall like old moth skin
and i will rise
like the scum that makes
the ground shimmer
to accept the acceptance
and raise an absentminded toast
to choose
outrage
over faith
and vanity is vanity
to cloth the emptiness of purity
only invisible can be pure
only invisible can be light
only invisible can bargain
with the devil
at the market

and i
and i
the olive skin
is yellow
yellow through the bones
while fucking white women for
the way they are not me

        awake awake
        you were crying again   what?
            the constellations, i say
        awake

and i
and i
a scissor to my ear
cutting open my prison
catching blood on a torn shirt
to rather be buried alive
in your mother's tomato garden
than be right
about the world

i am forgetting to clip my nails
the scratches on her back are parallel
her mouth filled with the bed sheet
she chews
and i am granted
another chance to fail
this knife in my hand

sometimes i mumble the words
like yellow
and yellowed
and the difference dancing
on papaya seeds

                            siamese twin spirals   the cluster of hercules
                                       why are you crying
                              her hand on my chest
                          9 degrees northeast of m13

and i
am a prelude
for the sparrow
in your womb
flapping like the great depression
and the slightest
hint
of heaven in flames

alleluia
and i
alleluia
and i

and there are seconds
when i am lightning
when i am fire
when i am crying
when i am gangrene

when i am peach
when i am shelter
when i am absolute
when i am porcelain
and there are seconds
when i am blood
when i am forced
when i am dry
when i am enough
when i am worth
when i am fear

                but see! as a swift ship
                    plows the waves
                        so does the monster come

                all these things

choose
alleluia
choose
despair

but nothing equal
to yesterday's sun
risen
fallen
like
twenty
and
twenty-one.

my heart, oh lord, touched with the words –

que vida!

and between the lines
there is infinite

and i said
father
father
pull me to sit behind you
on this black couch
as you rest
covered
in yellow paint
in yellow
covered
in yellow paint

selah

this good way
to walk in
to find a resting place
for these hands that grope
at pain
and all things
that rot

and all the people shall say—

christmas won't be christmas without any presents,

and tennyson speaks of bears
like hercules in summertime

        three steps
        leading

caught below the lion's jaw
this existence of a finite
contact resistance

do you like classical music?

        don't worry.
        they are not playing any
        stockhausen this summer.
        by the way, what is your name?

    the convection heat transfer coefficient
    may be determined
        by using newton's law
        of cooling

      canes venatici   as i consume myself
               whatever i am

oh, you mean my name?
oh, you mean—
selah

is it too late for the sun to go, the single crow
pecking at the brown dead of the lawn, this offer
at a glimpse of home, sixty two years to the day,
as i touch the wood, the wet wood, soaking me in.

we spoke then, his head tilted up to the ceiling,
sweat filling his wrinkles like so many unknown
rivers on his face, and she leaned in to get closer,
so i could hear, balancing with her hand on his left thigh.

she was so afraid. so afraid, of the inverse square
law of light propagation, she spoke then, rocking,
eyes from me to him then god, 93 million miles away.
she said, "who are you?" tightening the grip on his thigh.

raising my voice was the answer, loud enough to push
her back into the black couch, her red face, her wet eyes,
her lips that shake like winter romance, "mom," i said
and touched his hand to steal his skin. he looked at me.

what was it that we were going to say? and the ceiling,
and the street, and the crow, grant us this day, sixty
two years ago, how bright it was, like now, this day
in november, the sun wants to go, leave me on this wood.

i can cry now. it's okay. i can cry now because i have
exhaled through my disappointment, the dust beneath
his slipper cracking the soundtrack of my life,
this leg that won't heal. i can cry because i have raised my voice.

seeing the light that appeared so brief sixty two years ago,
like this sun, this sun, that goes too late –
i can cry now. we spoke then, stealing a square cut
of skin from his dying hand.

air, whiskey, breaths and wanting, so bright so bright
in the pain of his white shirt ruined with stucco.
i can cry the violence of micah, ordained in short
chapters that we preface with songs. 335. we sing. 402.

we sing, 89, 148, we sing, raising our voices.
i say mom, her fingers buried in his thigh, we will
never get better. i can cry now. i can
cry. trumpets. atonement. november 8. this year.

it's been so long. it's been so long. it's been so
long. it's been so long. it's been so long. amen.
it's been so long. amen. it's been so long. amen.
it's been so long—

perish everything
things
dismiss empty vanities

we know the reason
in our hands

          ed era una giornata calda
          ricordo piu tardi
          e gli occhi
          verdi

it's so dreadful to be poor,
she said

       tres meces
       olvidamos
       el rio
       y su cara

           of ghosts
           of grace
           falling -

                 it comes—
to walk
with two bright companions through
the milky way
i'm gone

         11 8 42
         6 30 38
         7 25 41
         12 11 66
         and one unforgettable
         august afternoon

and i said
i will pick
the grays from your head
until you are young enough
to make me
unborn
unattainable

kyrie

unattainable

halleluia

    open mouthed to the storm teeth buried in persimmon and oak, i commit treason when i cry because the wings are only remembered in the scent of blood, iguacu falls and the murders in brazil, they found them, two a week, korean men shot in the back of the head, and it only ended when i stopped listening about it, finding my boy cut in pieces in a dumpster in paraguay, i can only see the mango tree, leaning on my elbow, he was hiding under the brown buick station wagon, my eyes closed, counting to cuatro before the sap irritated my skin. the russians or the chinese, it's hard to tell, in little pieces, it's hard to tell.

    and my life my death electronically certified with numbers and letters and a misspelled name, i answer to the wrong calling when i recognize the voice, the summer of 89 and the return of the native, looking for cheap blankets at the street vendors, they scream, they scream at me, in my native tongue that embarrasses me, screaming korean hatred, cursing me back to america and cnn on the military channel, and thinking of jesus while stabbing them with my umbrella, thinking of jesus and the mysteries of love, thinking of jesus and what the fuck's he got to do with me.

unattainable

unattainable

fingers wrapped around heaven's throat

in the back of the train

praise him praise him

and at my window a curtain of yellow skin flapping in the hot breeze

and at my window equality in a clear plastic bag between the dog's teeth

and in my memory anticipating the tides and wild dogs with broken

 legs and wet pussies hanging full like lemons, the let down

and the slow swim

muting simply sentimental trembling

where are with one day cut

one day virgin

one day kneeling

broken i saying

terrified and nonchalant

the merciless the drowning the having nothing the stench of skin the
weight of skin breaking clavicles breaking faith the weight of skin breaking
jesus breaking jesus breaking jesus but what the fuck's he got to do –

and standing

at this edge of our failure

i hold the door open a woman with fair blonde hair

pushing triplets ahead of her, their faces stained like mine, nine
thousand dollars worth of babies that don't belong in her hands, and that
smile, that smile, oh my heart is steadfast, god, my heart is steadfast, that
smile, i will shoot it with arrows, suddenly it will be struck down, i will turn
her tongue against her and bring her to ruin, and all who see her hands on
such yellow skin will shake their heads in scorn.

and standing

at this edge of our failure

a poem in my hand words chipped off the bones of ezra, sliced from
the heart of cesaire, i wear these pages like a cloak, make myself super-
hero, the invisible, the transparent man, the skinless man, but they recog-
nize my smell, they recognize my eyes, and i am nothing but—like that
other—

that we are the same

that we should greet each other on wilshire in passing

that we should change our names

and when the heat matures into storm

i will tear blonde hair off pail scalps

and decorate my garden

each time a chink baby is bought

to be given useless names like james

stain their flesh with my distant soil

until they're forced to wash themselves

with me

in the same piss

                   it comes now father

                   like you said

                              the end of us

                              the eternity

            selah

and at this edge of our failure

standing

in front of my father

my body becoming as large as his
his left arm cut open with a saw
cutting my left ear open
squeezing the blood out
squeezing the puss out
squeezing out everything we share
on the floor
on my footsteps
to wash away every trace
of my journey.

    we lose alone

72 10N
1 121   109

       from toil and dread...
and i said -

        what?

and god said
       i will give you the wings you pray for
       but nobody can make it across the ocean
and god said
       you snakes! you brood of vipers!
       how will you escape?

and god said

        in the time of my favor

        in the day of salvation

and god said

        come out   be free

and he said

        nothing, just looking at your face.

        you look like your uncle.

and god said

        5128 5139 6960 6962

        2903 3190 3623 as the night grows warmer

and god said

        the honeysuckle the horror

        who will comfort thee -

            in an emptying room

            6 28

            he calls me by name

            and

            i say father

            my outstretched arms

            mine

            adding the sails to the ships

        and all the people shall say

                    amen

        and all the people shall say

                    amen

and all the people shall say

        amen

and all the people shall say

        amen

and all the people shall say

        amen

and all the people shall say

        halleluia

and all the people shall say

        amen

and all the people shall say

        amen

        amen

        amen

        amen

and all the people shall say

        amen

and all the people shall say -

consider
variations of this
and wanting for more radiance
the sun over gibeon that day
risk being lied to to touch
the scar on her neck
that reaches across the wooden table
past orion
below the fourth rib
atonement waiting on a plate made of bones

where it is voiceless
and a face stained with cherry ice cream
and the black marks
in the shape of fingertips
down her back
and her ass
we hold on so tight
to such things we want to annihilate

                    put a foot down on the asphalt
                    137 degrees
                    call it home
                    and breathe

          behold i too say
        for like the grass

       un solo muerto en el agua
           no more of this, said jesus

     awake next to her
     the tanks on grand avenue
     the blood on 6th

             blessed is he in the course of time

in spring
never was there a stranger

adio sospetti
        and naked eye views
        scattered like chaff
        this lot
        this portion
        all decreed

        not quite .5 degrees
the swan's neck   less than i

and six faint naked
forming a semi-circle
and i stand by the fence
as the neighbor crosses the street
shaking hands
as i ask of him a favor
and he nods
and joy discovered the tenth
the sea
a golden ram
sound the trumpet, o destroyer

        well yes well yes
        i think we better be cutting along

    as a man comes
    so he never -

        virgine mio cor -

and wanting for light
in mexican-irish green eyes
and polish tits too expensive to suck
and she says
my pussy is this small
making a circle
with her thumb and index finger
like she is saying okay
but not okay
you can eat out my ass
in the dark

                      i think the country won't change
                      for a long time

          blue giant evolved
          perseus delivers andromeda

          kyrie

this dark obscuration
considered
and wanting
in righteousness and truth
in this quest for the sunrise
as god hangs mom by her feet for the storm

                108
                94
                23

and shame
and all the women dead
sisters daughters unborn mothers

the thin-walled promise
of sweaty hands

and yet
considered
november 8, 1942
there was brightness
illuminata
seeking radiance
or a little more
lalalalala

let us run from it
it is better to die alone
on the large cloud
1.5 degrees

arm reaching over the black fence
he nods
and fernando speaks
i'll keep an out on your parents
any stranger around here
i'll come out with my guns firing
and i thank him

for the director of music
a psalm

la luna
mi voz
cieno
amargo

in my hands
broken
the shells of your judgment
covered in blood
disregard me

consider
variations of
wanting light
in the corner
we forget she is just a whore
and i forget everything else
the words
these are

spiritu
spiritu

and in this moment
there is enough courage in spite
to speak exactly the words
that mean my life

dwelling lofty quasar caballo
given 2244 south
cross rosetta
held unripe
ixion
war   sarah   at   six   the light
                                        the light
                                        the light

and on my ceiling
the universe not there
his foot shuffling dust
            let me know—

and in the backyard
the blind dog memorize her new surrounding with small steps
counting the bricks that pass under her feet
and turn and three steps and turn

            let me know thee, o lord, as i am known

and i prayed for the ability to love my life
and god answered me
and he took my father and propped him up on an old scarecrow
and god poisoned my father's blood
then took his eyes
and i stood in front of my old man

and god said next will be his kidney and his bones
and there will not be one moment in which he doesn't die
surely you will watch him for the rest of it
like a good son
and i said, i have prayed to you
and fell to my knees
and he said, will you love your life now

and the things
i remember
will fill me with regret

          of ghosts
          of grace
          su sangre

     6   3192   2623
     small lion
     what was there last month

     and it's funny

just behind the bear's ears
7 million years
distant.
         her breathing
         her head on my arm

we are distant.
we are distant.
we are so apart.

                    so...so...

selah

and the foot of the cross is defined
love must be sincere
more than rubies
more that the shifting of our eyes

i am a beggar
with burnt hands
erasing my name
from the things that i hold

        oh men of israel

                        and all the people shall say -
the lens
the slippers
the blaze
the damage
the dates marked in blue
the straw cross
the lost pages
the dried orange peel
that letter

those promises
these coins

and this
this the remains of a toothless fantasy
this lost heap in a cavern of bones
this fist in black paint searching for god
this is the water of mercy
this is yellow photo album from the last days of access
this is the edge of my failure
this is the edge of my skin
this is my final acceptance of grace
this is my final scream

alleluia
alleluia
to the god of daniel
alleluia
to the lions in the den
alleulia
mene mene tekel parsin
motherfucker

and i'm frightened to keep what i have and alleluia to his name and
not listening, not listening, deaf enough to believe in the future when the
present is a mid-life crisis, and this skin, my skin, in wanting something
other than my life, my father loves this song, he asks for it day and night,
wants to know what the words mean as his fake teeth break and fall out of
his mouth.

it's of love
it's about love
of love
when not listening
of love
when not loving

and i'm frightened to keep what i have, not listening, not listening, because nobody talks, nobody says anything, easy or otherwise, that beauty is the scar on my wrist and everything else fails, and i was guessing, my arms wrapped around his left leg, the way the woman in the white pumps looked at him, how i could feel him shifting his weight, how i closed my eyes, guessing that this was sleep, the serpent hanging from the noose of my shame as he grants me this moment, half asleep, shaking on my underdeveloped bird legs, mouth shut not to cry, trembling, grants me this moment of manhood.

and i'm falling
and i'm loving
and i'm hiding
and i'm frightened
of the lions
of the violin
of the clock
of the dark hallway
of the hole in his left arm
of the way he squints so hard when he tries to read the mail from medi-cal
of the way he walks through the aisles at costco with such purpose

but enough of this story
enough of such sentiment
this is where the piano begins a new disappointing song
this is the edge of my failure
this is the edge of my mask

and the sun beats down
as we drive through koreatown

                  to his house

                      the porch

            my hands on the wet wooden bench

              dust under his shoe

    pointing at pollo alla brasa on eighth and western

    and at the sushi place on oxford where the chef was shot in the face

    and the video store on ninth where the clerk was shot in the chest

    and the liquor store owner who left two angry sons behind and a pile
of cash hidden under the bed before he went and got himself shot

    and the geography of my life i

    marked by kentucky fried chickens and dead koreans

    and my sister in law's father who was killed in the supermarket for a
few bills—he was korean too.

    as dead.

    as meaningless.
neither black nor white.
the coward. chose to stay yellow.

but why do i scream.

                          awake awake
                                   stymphalian birds
                                             i got you, my love   oh my love
                          her voice
                          amen

this is the edge
and tonight i could be skinless
because i'm sitting across from my brother
37 in december
wondering why the divorce papers haven't been finalized
telling me that he doesn't know what to do with his life
that he is having a mid-life crisis
that his doctor tells him to change his diet
that he needs to quit his job
do something else
figure out what to do
as his soon to be ex-wife backpacks across europe

and none of this matters
and i'm frightened of nothing
except his face
his cheeks a bit fatter
his plastic front tooth getting more purple and crooked
the tooth he lost when the front wheel of his bicycle
hit the pothole camouflaged in old rain water
and how my mother knew his life would be difficult
          but not like this
and how she knew my life would be blessed

but not like this
because i am not ready for grace
                              unattainable
i am not ready for blessings
i am not ready to be saved.

because you'd think that after 18 years of writing
this would get easier, but it doesn't.
maybe it's cuz i got more stuff going on in my head and more stuff
that i'm feeling.
when i was 17, the only thing to write about was living and dying,
as in should i.

but now? i'm looking through books to prepare a lesson for the
compton students tomorrow.
so tomorrow i'll be reading cesaire and tu fu and bill shields to 12
through 18 year olds, show them what it is to write
a poem that can rip someone apart in 36 pieces,
a poem that can fill the rivers with blood,
poetry that chooses to kill, not save.

and this bone that rips through my chest is the rage today, reading of
hot 97 new york city and the dj saying he's gonna start shooting asians and
the tsunami songs about screaming chinks and selling asian orphans into
slavery or adoption, miss jones miss jones and the silent leaders, millions
of listeners listening and new york times doesn't care.

today i will no longer call myself a poet because i am too busy wishing
them all dead.

i am angry because—

       selah

waking up at 1 a.m., staring into the ceiling
she's tossing next to me
and the dogs were barking
and at 5
we heard my father running down the stairs
we heard him fall down the stairs
    unattainable

       kyrie

    unattainable

       halleluia

i heard him in pain
i heard him grow old
i heard him in darkness
i heard him living
i heard him dying
i heard him hold in his scream with his toothless mouth
i heard him call my name
i heard him wishing he'd raised me well
i heard his regret
i heard him fail
i heard him missing a step again
i heard him miss
he heard me hide
he heard me scared
and i am angry because my father is falling
falling in front of my eyes when i can't sleep
and they say it was a full moon last night but i know better now

that it's not the full moon.
it's still nothing more than this simple choice between—

206,265
            3.26

            each y
            the inverse square law of light propagation

    -26.78
            a more modest
            2.0

2.523 times more
the fifth root of 100   and november 8, 1942

                    93 million miles apart

        ngc 253
        sculpting in its studio
it is to want
to be born
        at 110 kpc

                    ngc 55   3.6 degrees
                        north northwest

and you are so bright
in your pain
and i see him too
   i see him too
so careful in his
white shirt

       psalm 15
       lev 16

           23:26-32
           29:7-11

               7th month

               3:24-26
               9:7   10:3   19-22

           plowing in the beginning
           of the autumn rain

      trumpets
      atonement
      tabernacles

                   perpetuo socorro
                   in 4th grade

and this epic of creation
god's palace on the milky way
his plan backfired
because it is too easy to love this life
and he left her
in the sky
north and east of insects

     ra 22 h 03 m   delta –00 degrees 34'

   m 2.93
       the lucky one of the king

       she is the sky
       and beauty for once
       does not degenerate

              o lord
              i am thy servant
              i am thy servant
              i am thy servant
              i am the son
              of thy handmade joke
              i lick the thorn
              in my side
              in my flesh
              and it is sweet

        in f-sharp minor

and this is the edge of our failure, the wet heart of a cave and the regrets hieroglyphed with dry splintered bones, sho-nuf, that thing you whispered in your sleep last night, two cross-my-hearts and waiting to feed the famine with dead whores – hitting the earth like an invasion – such silent nights without symphonies.

all the bottles lie emptiness, such trees hung from red strings and choked off from yearn, i write a letter, i write a letter before the after to know why i am leaving, my feet buried in pickled skin and pork dumplings, the 85% of real, the ice melting in whiskey to escape the radiation, i write a letter promissory in nature because i'm a criminal by nature, a killer by nature, a rapist by nature, drunk by nature, these words meaning nothing by nature, beauty by nature, a carrier by nature, to spread armageddon by nature, yellow by nature, olive to some, blind cocksucker.

and this is the edge of our failure, the message from a blocked number, "i ought to fucken shoot you for sticking that shit down my throat like that after fucking my ass," it says, but we love each other, right right?

and this is the edge of our failure, the fruitless garden on crying out from the darkness of mom's wrinkles and the centrifugal force of the white earth spinning on a table top like george washington.

and this is the edge of our failure dancing, shaking, blowing dicks on figueroa street to murder music.

another day born from self adhesion and breaking the world with an infantry of generic ideas...

water in scotch, water in whiskey, we are useless in an endless variety of flavors.

another day born, calligraphy without interpretation, beautifying meaningless words, passports expiring in april, this is the trap, this is the trap, and i am called the other, the other, she says the other like she knows me, ash stained forehead in the shape of a cross, or an X, or the spot that marks ignorance, calling me the other while looking at the hudson river from her washington square apartment, the other like she knows this knife in my pocket will open up her dried up cunt so she can fuck the running elephant that chases me through my house, through my dream, since i was 6, so she can give birth to herself, so much younger, make her see what she no longer is, young, wanting, desired, correct.

and this is the edge of our failure, the edge of my skin, the edge of my other, the edge of my yellow, the edge of the only thing i know, the edge of my country, my shelter, my concentration camp, the edge of your permission.

another day born to die, the little glitch in the master plan, the security envelope addressed to the last petal of a tiger orchid, and the heart in a wooden frame waiting to pulse, astronomy, chemistry, bible, and the elements of materials and feedback control.

give me the music

give me no frills

give me white pussy shaved to fuck like my dick in your babygirl and the nightmare that will never end

give me one second and another

give me the rain the hurricane read my lips the water the curtain closed flapping two times quick to the jugular to the artery that pain in your chest my name carved careless and true

give me a cup with a broken handle

give me red lights at this intersection

give me black giraffes and a matchbox and the lifeline from the palm of your right hand

give me jesus made from sand and explicit lyrics

give me a chance to take everything

and this is the edge

and this is the edge of failure painted on my chest like a bird, like nothing new, at 6:45 waiting for rice and water for flavor, the other, this other, finding myself, on point, privacy in veil, bottom of an empty box, and line 3 on the selection form, real world range testing and knowledge of destruction, the necessary strength and the joyful life on westchester place, the anointing, morphed and abstract, it provides, trampled and hatred, it provides.

mi soledad
la tierra
buscabas

and birth

the demon
among the stars
shining
as bright

i am healing the crippled
you see?

the loud tide
and her rugged hands
don't want the weight of my arms

like a unicorn crouching by orion

i speak to god in accents

of rocks melting
in scotch
burning
psalm 132

and the afterlife -

she said
this is the treasure
to know

and all the people shall say -

i saw him
i saw him while i was standing in the living room
on the edge of the rug
by the coffee table
saw him rubbing his fingers together
i finished the glass of water
and looked down
at him sitting
and i said -

the manifestation of original power
like fire
the splitting of atom
like fear
like trembling
some time ago -

52:7

how good are the feet on the mountains

     and one day
     and one night
     staying where there is happiness

fingers
rubbed
air
caught
nothing
    and seeing
i saw
this man
water
finished
crossing
he said -

24:15   not one will be left

this world destroyed
the origin
hiroshima
   my love

and the birch tree bending...
oh you know which way and what!

six faint naked-eye stars
and hercules in a dress
a fine one
like a lady

i stand behind him
his shirt sticking to his back
white fabric stained with spackle
and wood shavings
gray hair wet on his scalp
and the scent of his sweat
is a question i can't ask

shivering
when my bones are covered
in dew
when does the winter come
as the yellow dies in the sun

columnas de cieno

how it no longer looks alive
dead and dying like our skin
yellow
and she puts her hands on her hips
and he puts his hands in his pockets

and i scratch three letters
and four numbers on my arm
with my uncut nail

      and neruda writes the words love and clouds
      in the same fucking cheeseball line
      what a fucking con

         bought from a raven
            from the red bricks
        the blade unclean
               and it was something about
                    crumbling

      the fucking cunt never wanted
      to talk about the real

and in the early morning
it was early morning
god did tempt abraham
and nothing has been the same

         at 300k and 1mm porous sphere
         consider the use of kerosene
         and the three tragic myths

      we are ocean
      we are sky
      we are earth

my hands on his neck
slipping on his fatigue
i place them on his shoulders
tangle my finger on the wet shirt
a little to the side, he says
and i push,
a little more, he says
and i push

my legs tingle and go numb, he says
and i can't tell him i am too much like him
that my own legs are dying.

you'll be an expert healer when we're done, he says
as i walk to the kitchen sink and wash my hands with soap
and go back one last time
put my hands on his back one last time
and shatter into pieces
          fragments
  stars   ngc 6514
            ngc 1976
            m332   job 38:31   20'
ngc 3587   m81   ngc6822   monoceros

          pulsating
             m67 epsilon   ngc 2903   3190

   thumbprints on his skin   m57 the hunters
          summer 4486

m104ngc 2237   regretting
7 degrees ssw
                    ngc 5272

make me extraordinary
and i will accept without rebellion
without the chalice of piss
make me equal
and i will sleep in your narrow shadow
and the ocean with ruffled feathers
clip and oil
that ties me at the ankles held together with glue and crossed fingers
this last geography
this measurement of apocalypse
running out of numbers like running out of rosaries
this inevitable room and the circular cold snap.

my country on television
my home on television
my origin on television
all going to hell in little fast cars
the faces the duplicity the recognition
cut from the same sheet of tanned leather wrapped tight over bamboo
skeletons
the width of cheeks
the eyes drowned in shallow waters
the contours i remember at the tips of my curled fingers
it all goes to hell

and i am not sacred

the beauty

the castle built on parasite shells like

good luck that never dies and the flowers for inner healing

the golden rod the pretty face and other unknown events

and i am not sacred

       nor just begun suddenly when black is evil and white the rule where

do i bury my small feet

       yellow as the deathbed of grandpa an old man deserving of death for

sure even in his last more pleasant shade of blue.

there was yellow that night

there was yellow in the sky

there was yellow in the explosions

there was yellow fading and gone

there was yellow going to hell.

and standing at farmers market on larchmont sunday morning

the tomatoes don't ripen in my hands

and tomorrow we will park empty cars in this space

at the edge of our failure

carrying prayers and grandchildren in fancy bags

walking running moving our feet fast enough not on the ground long enough

to grow roots to plant ourselves

to wait for the hard rain to let the fruits rip through our flesh

i see you woman

your face like mine

i know where you come from

my parents ran ahead of yours across the border when the reds came
they watched the handshake between white men
as they cut our land in half and shared it like a smooth expensive dessert
i see you woman
you will not shed your skin
you will not cleanse yourself from the sin of pigmentation

and i have tried
and i have tried

unripe tomatoes in my hand
my dick buried between pale thighs
looking down each time i pulled it out
hoping for more than disappointment.

and this
firewalker ants and scotch rings on the glass
and this
this sunday morning
unripening
unmake me
at
this edge of our failure
at this edge of our failure
make me extraordinary
rest me in a parcel headed to jerusalem
make me—

this is the sun
this is the day

             and this night that doesn't even begin

and of the things
i remember
they will be filled with regret

    and i was wondering –

    an idea stuck between two endings, crawling toward each other's miseries skin wet from mist, the garbage flying like moths in the wind, keep your eyes shut, son, keep your eyes shut, son, the dust from moth wings will blind you, ugly boy, at 3:42 a.m. and kicking a black and white ball harder than this fist, son –

    still wondering

    who will stand under the grandstand in pants made of cool white fabric to wave his hat and send me back when i arrive, jump off the flying saucer my mother made with a hammer and her two hands during a hot july when nobody remembered that she was born, aliens and all, and a hook to hang my hat that she always thought made my face look big. who will kneel down with a chalk in her hand when i get to number 372 in my list of places to touch, making lines on the ground until i am dead enough to fit snug within. who will peel his face from his head, sprinkled with mustard seeds, tear off my shirt and stitch it to my chest, keep it shut, son, move the empty bottles, son, get your ass home, son –

    i will go
    and i will go
    and i will get to number 373
    and i will go

tie myself around the oak tree
become something that grows
with girth mystical divine smolder
like painting myself with better flavor
the edge of our failure...
i am named in the wrinkle of shame like pixels and dust
i am named in the headstone of a fatman's next life
i am named in the dried blood on a green towel
i am named bear
i am named with difficult syllables

mistrusted blue mornings
empty shells rolling toward the curb
forgiveness in slow movements
salvation in slow movements
transformation in slow movements
i am named in the space inside the fingers of your fist
and tell me that you don't see my skin
the moth wings over your bed
the dust in your eyes
when the dream ended too early
it's difficult to remember commands in sleep
it's difficult to remember where to stand
and tell me that you don't see my skin
and i will place my hands on your useless eyes
bring enough vision
make all things visible
this knife in my hand
the teeth in my smile

the rape in my kiss
and the swift left right motion and straight in
your lonely soul pulsing
on the oil stained concrete of a gas station

and in the edge of our failure
two peaches and a snail
and cutting tumors off with orange handled scissors
and ah
ah
ah
so long infant toes curling in mid air
so long declarations of love to a scar on her side
so long father
so long mother
so long stained flesh
because
i am ashamed to call no land my home
i am ashamed of these borrowed words
these learned words
these foreign words
beautiful and weightless
strung together like pearls
strung together like rotten garlic
strung together like stolen bones
these ugly words
that name me
with difficult syllables
and faint shadows.

and if i scream
each time i scream in the night
she wakes up and shakes me
to tell me that i am not alone
but the nights
stay dark
and he is there—

and i hope
that we can still
after all this
after the pain it has brought to
us

                    end this at one
                    there is no need
                    and to stay
and something else too

                                        blunted
                                        in solitude
                                        goodness

and of this magic
between us
we have built so much of our homes
on hatred
we will withstand the hurricane
we are unmistakably human
vowing

(and of this magic
between us
the dead father and the mother dying
we have built so much of our homes
on hatred
and the garden is thriving
and we will withstand the hurricane
and she marked page 59
in such small black letters
we are unmistakably human
vowing
and i kissed her close to the left ear
moving closer and closer
as she spoke
close to the left corner of her mouth
so close
and she made a vow
in my arms
that we will one day
kill each other)

                    this revolving
               chemical and trembling
                                   such intricate symbolic order
                   selected
            and ease of use was
                         of self knowledge
               how tall he's become
             as true is good
            and

may mayo the funeral dirt

springs eternal

and after

oh fuck

perfect for one night

peeled

cumming inside this strangeness
and the spatula on the pan
and the boiled water cooling

60 seconds to the southeast of beta
lies the most famous example

i am terrified
and if i was strong enough
to leave this bed again
i would speak
of fourteen generations
and my brother's eyes
that refused to see me born
and chose blindness
they came back
his eyes
when i fell head first
off his desk

and the spiral galaxy around me showing
a dark obscuration of dust and matter

and hercules first slay
the gigantic nemean lion
while they pierce my skin
with iron

then all the people shall say   amen

amen

born of a tired hunter
who only wanted to relive the day

after the exile

born to the hope
of being called christ one day

she looks me in the eyes and says
oh all the young minds you must have corrupted
with pieces of squid in chilli paste stuck between her teeth

on november 8, 1942
that day again
north northeast of zeta

but what about choice

are we now adding sails to our ship

yes mother
that's why i was born of it, observed jo

no longer visible
by the end of the month

      naked as my eye
      forty two years old in a doorway
      scar on her side
      telling her i'll kill her
      if she keeps loving me

and somewhere the maze
      begat
          a record   to

      abraham to isaac to jacob
      to judah to perez to zerah
      to hezron to ram to amminadab
      to nashon to salmon to boaz
      to obed and somewhere rahab and ruth
      to fyodor pavlovich to alexei his third
      to mitya the gone to maury to benji
      to quentin to caddy to lear
      to edgar to edmund to banquo to lady mac
      to seymore to buddy to boo boo to franny
      to harry white and tralala to georgette
      to new jersey to brooklyn to marion to
      tyrone c to jo to meg to mother and robert

to akim to eliud to eleazar to matthan
to jacob to joseph to mary to

and i put my hand
on her stomach,
feel the rise and fall,
not holy enough to bless anything,
dying in the terror of the sun that will come
until i am blind enough
to see
its beauty.

and all the people shall say

november 8, 1942 -
suddenly appearing -
one of the brightest -

faded very quickly -

no longer visible -

by the end of the month...